Michael Nyman

Four Ostinatos

for Solo Bass Clarinet

(1979/2013)

1. Bird List Song 1
2. Drawing II: days 4 and 5 6
3. Mouth to Mouth 8
4. Melody Lists 10

Four Ostinatos

arranged for Solo Bass Clarinet

MICHAEL NYMAN
Edited by Andy Keenan

1. Bird List Song

V.S.

2. Drawing II: days 4 and 5

3. Mouth to Mouth

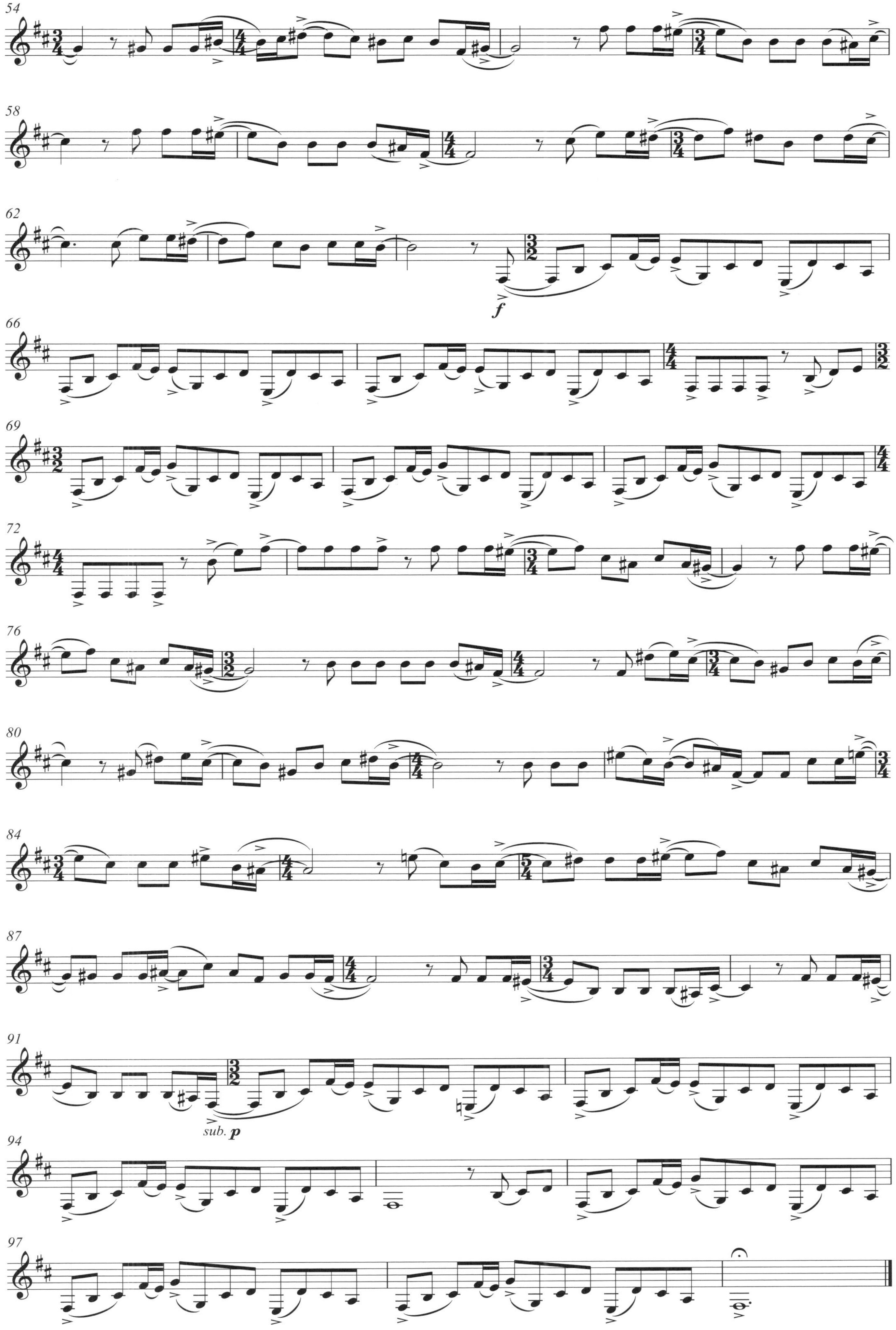
54
58
62
f
66
69
72
76
80
84
87
91
sub. ***p***
94
97

4. Melody Lists

Instructions for performance: Each 8 bar phrase to be repeated a number of times at the discretion of the player.

V.S.

12

FINE